E
Broadcasting

BREAKING
INTO
Broadcasting

The Fast Track to Landing Your First or Next On-Air Job in Television

by TOM ZENNER and JON KELLEY

Printed in the United States of America.

This book is available in quantity at special discounts.
For more information contact:
The KasterZ Co.
P.O. Box 6824
Aurora, IL 60598
www.broadcastingjobs.com
(630)292-4261

ISBN 0-9655895-0-1

CREDITS

WRITTEN BY
Tom Zenner and Jon Kelley

COVER AND BOOK DESIGN BY
Mulligan plus Mulligan Design

FRONT COVER PHOTOGRAPHY BY
Linda Schwartz

WEB SITE DESIGN
Internet Presence Coordinators

PRINTING BY
Graphic Arts Studio

Acknowledgements

To my mother Peggy Kelley. Thank you for teaching me and preaching the fine arts of writing and communicating. Your passion for life has become my passion. All my success is your success. **JK**

We would like to thank everyone who inspired us and provided the resources to bring this project to life. It is something we have talked about doing for a long time, and our thanks to the countless friends, family members, loved ones, college professors, advisors and colleagues who encouraged us, started us on the path we now travel, and kept us focused and pointed in the right direction. **TZ**

Table of Contents

Introduction
PAGE ix

Introduction

Welcome to the world of television broadcasting. Obviously, the reason you picked up this book is because you want to be on TV. You've made up your mind. You want a challenging and rewarding career. A high profile, action-packed gig. The kind of job many people want and dream about, but few actually know how to get. And even fewer understand the **BEST WAYS TO MAKE THIS DREAM A REALITY.**

To break it down into its simplest form, television broadcasting is about communicating: talking to people, telling stories, giving information and entertaining along the way. It all sounds so simple to do, and admit it, you've sat in front of the tube watching some kind of broadcast and said, "That's not so tough, I CAN DO THAT."

Hey, we're not about to tell you that what we do is brain surgery, because it certainly isn't. But it does take a special talent to make it in this fiercely competitive field. To do this, you'll need to be armed with every single edge possible. And because you are already holding this book, you've got a great head start on an exciting future.

What you are about to dive into is a guide to pursuing an ON-AIR career in television broadcasting. Inside you will find a proven game plan for landing your first or next job in TV, and also ways to advance in your career.

What we share with you in the following chapters HAS WORKED FOR US, and if you apply what you learn with passion and commitment, IT WILL WORK FOR YOU. Remember, we were in your shoes not too long ago.

We both agree that one of our biggest professional thrills was landing our first jobs. As we have advanced in our careers, we now get questions every day from people like you wanting to know how we got into the business, and asking what steps we took to develop a successful career. And that's why we decided to put down on paper everything we've been preaching, including our own personal experiences, (good and bad), tips and secrets from SOME OF THE TOP NAMES IN THE INDUSTRY, and proof that energy and attitude go hand in hand with talent.

Basically, we put together the kind of book that will not only answer all your questions, but just as importantly, show you how to jump onto THE FAST TRACK TO LANDING YOUR FIRST OR NEXT ON-AIR JOB IN TELEVISION.

We wish you the best of luck in your pursuits, and we hope our book will play a part in getting you where you want to be. Enjoy the book, and we will see YOU on the air.

The College Experience: Getting a Jump

*"Think of yourself as on the threshold of
unparalleled success. A whole, clear, glorious life lies before you.
Achieve! Achieve!"*

ANDREW CARNEGIE

Unlike some of your friends who are pursuing careers in engineering, architecture, medicine or any other profession for that matter, you won't learn how to become a success in broadcasting merely from what you learn in the classroom. For one thing, a communications or broadcasting degree is not even required to get an on-air TV job. We both know many people in this industry with backgrounds in several different areas, and the reality is a good number of them had no communications background at all.

As far as a college education goes, we highly suggest one, but unless you make the most of it and gain every possible edge, let's face it, your degree will be nothing more than a piece of paper. Even though plenty of people kid themselves, that piece of paper doesn't guarantee or assure anything but something to hang on your wall.

If the school you are attending has a broadcasting or communications program, we recommend you take as many classes as you can in that area. You may choose to major or minor with a degree in that as well. But the best thing about college, and preparing for a career in television, is getting a WELL ROUNDED education. Take classes in all fields. Whether you have aspirations to work in news, weather, sports or entertainment, don't limit yourself. For example, take as many English, writing, history and foreign language classes as possible. Believe us, the more diverse your education is, the better prepared you will be to handle the challenges you will face when you start your career.

Another thing you might not think of is the benefit of acting classes, especially the impromptu ones. These provide great opportunities for you to enhance those ad-libbing skills you will need. Why not get the stage fright out of the way so you don't sweat through your suit the first time you go on the air, like both us did in our forgettable debuts? (This will save you some embarrassment, not to mention a few bucks at the dry cleaners.)

And do keep in mind, while all classes related to broadcasting and communications help you get rolling toward a career, and while it makes sense to be committed to these types of courses, **you'll need to go far beyond what your instructors teach during a semester to get a real edge.**

Here are some quick tips on what kind of things can get you set for a job on television:

Speech Courses

We can't stress this enough. Take a high volume of speech courses because the more you take the better prepared you will be for getting in front of the camera. These are great because they teach you how to gather and research information, put it into a format, and deliver it smoothly and in a polished fashion.

Take as many as your schedule allows. Trust us, being relaxed, comfortable, and conversational is half the battle when you're sitting in front of that camera.

Writing Courses

Many people overlook the fact that great broadcasting begins with great writing. Along with being comfortable in front of that camera, you have to be able to put that story into words, YOUR WORDS. The only way to master this craft is to become a solid writer and learn to write how you speak. You will find as you go along, sometimes things that look slick on paper don't translate into a smooth line when it comes out of your mouth.

Interviewing Courses

Most colleges offer some sort of class like this. They are extremely advantageous, because they teach you techniques to become a solid interviewer who can think on the move. The other key to interviewing classes is that they also teach you the art of the JOB INTERVIEW. We will get into this heavily in later chapters.

Practice Reading Out Loud

Yeah, you might feel silly doing this, and people may give you grief if they catch you doing it, but so what! Who cares if it seems weird reading out loud, because it's the best way to find your speech rhythm.

You have a rhythm in everything you do (some have more than others, of course, but fortunately, we're not talking about dancing).—the way we walk, the way we talk, the way our eyes and facial expressions move, and the way we breathe. You can read just about anything out loud: newspapers, magazines, letters, cereal boxes, the graffiti on the inside of bathroom stalls. Whatever.

The key is developing a smooth reading flow and learning how to read without stumbling. No, it won't be in your own writing, so it will be tough at times. But if you can get comfortable reading things that aren't in your words, imagine how much stronger you will be when they actually are.

As far as friends and people snickering and giving you funny looks when they find you reading out loud, we promise they will stop when you're on television, and they are at home watching!

Make Contacts with People In the Business You Admire

This is one of the easiest, but least thought-of moves to make. Just pick up the phone and call a local broadcaster you admire. (You can also try to contact national broadcasters, but it's easier to meet with people who work in or close to the city where you live).

Let them know you dig their work, pick their brains, find out how they made it, and try to set up a time when you can go to the station and shadow them for a day or two on the job. (We said shadow, not stalk.) Most times, people are flattered and more than happy to share their "wisdom." This is a classic way to see what the job is really like.

Be persistent, while at the same time courteous. Keep in mind, those people you call are working. We've had our share of people who become a pain in the butt and try to take advantage of the situation. And if someone you call is rude, arrogant or just a plain jerk, don't sweat it. You don't want to learn from a clown like that anyway.

Watch and Learn, but Don't Imitate

There is nothing wrong with learning from talented people in television. Obviously, they've done something right to get where they are. Watch closely and pick up what you like and don't like about their style. But, when you finally get a chance to go on, avoid trying to "be" the person or people you admire.

Learn from their skills, draw from what they do, but find a way to make what you learn from them work with your own personality. You may not want to believe it, but most people who watch television are smart enough to figure out who seems "natural and real," versus a person who seems like they are forcing something, or simply trying to be someone they're not. Chill out, relax, figure out who and what you're about in everyday life. You'll want to find a way to translate your normal personality onto the screen.

In simple terms, if you are a funny person, then it's perfectly acceptable to use your natural humor on the air. (Remember, there is a big difference between actually "being" funny, and "thinking" you are funny.) Don't fake something you are not. Phony people are big-time turnoffs, and that's what viewers do to them: TURN THEM OFF.

Next, we touch on one of the most important parts of the college experience (the parties). Actually we mean the on-air experience you get at campus radio and television stations. Most universities don't have television stations, but almost all have radio stations that broadcast throughout the day. Make it a point to see the manager of the station in your freshman year, (or right now if you are an upperclassman). Any early experience you can get behind the microphone or in front of the camera will prepare you for the future.

Volunteer to read the news live, on-air whenever a slot is available. That means doing it early in the morning when normally you would still be hugging your pillow, or even a late night graveyard shift. And if there's a chance to work as a DJ on the campus station, jump at the opportunity. This type of work is a blast, it will force you to bring out your personality on the air and get you comfortable performing.

When you get a chance to get some on-air work, make it a point to ALWAYS WRITE YOUR OWN COPY. Don't get in the habit of having someone else write for you, or simply ripping and reading wire copy. That is the quick and easy way out, it develops terrible habits, and it will not help you get ahead in this business. And if you have aspirations of becoming a sportscaster, get involved in any special sports programming your campus station may offer.

For those of you who don't have access to doing "live" work, here's a killer tip: find a tape recorder and read stories into it. You can read copy you have written, do weather forecasts, critique movies, or even go to local sporting events and do play by play or commentary. When you've compiled some tapes, listen and critique them yourself, and also seek out professionals in broadcasting to give you feedback. A tape recorder will be available almost any time and any place, and as often as your vocal chords will allow. Talking and listening to yourself on tape is a great exercise, and really, the only thing holding you back is some fresh batteries.

If your school is lacking in television facilities, don't worry, there are still plenty of ways to get in front of a camera. When Tom was attending school there was a local cable access station that allowed students to produce and air a weekly 30 minute newscast. This may sound a little intimidating for someone with little or no experience, and you may even feel uncomfortable trying to pull something like this off. But what it actually amounts to is a bona fide TV experience, and you should take advantage of opportunities like this.

Tom eventually put together a weekly variety segment, and while he thought it was witty, irreverent, and cutting edge humor at the time, he looks back now and cringes. But despite any embarrassment that may have gone with it, his cable access show gave him some invaluable experience producing and creating something new and fresh on a regular basis.

Make it a priority to contact any local public or cable access TV and/or radio stations. Find out what kind of opportunities may be available to you. Don't expect to be paid, because you probably won't be. At this point in your career, money should not be the main focus. Any and all experience you soak up will be more than worth the effort.

College Years
R E V I E W

Get the most
well-rounded education possible.

Load up
on writing, speech and acting classes.

Go above and beyond
the call of duty to apply what you learn.

Start making contacts
with the pros and learn from them
about their craft.

Find out
what kind of practical
experiences you can start attaining at radio
and television stations.

Internships

"Success is the reward for accomplishment."

HARRY F. BANKS

For most people this is where the REAL EDUCATION TAKES PLACE. We both found that internships at a television station are far and away the best chance to learn what this business is all about. Internships allow you to get directly involved in the broadcasting business and get an understanding of what you're really getting into.

When we get on the topic of internships, it blows us away to hear how many students either ignore them or don't have a clue how important they really are. DO NOT PASS UP AN OPPORTUNITY AT AN INTERNSHIP. The reality is, while many people will be more excited about a broadcasting career when the internship is all over, others will figure out they do not enjoy the grind, deadlines, pressure, and everything that goes along with this wild and unpredictable world of television.

The following is a list of pros and cons of a broadcast internship:

Pros

- Great for learning and understanding what goes on behind the scenes.
- Provides real life "hands-on" experience.
- Allows you to watch the professionals do what you hope to do in the near future.
- Allows you to pick up different traits from a variety of people.
- Provides the opportunity (if you are aggressive) to get some work on tape.
- Gives you a shot at learning "secrets" and behind the scenes information.
- Allows you the chance to establish important contacts and do some networking.
- Provides a wide open opportunity to take the internship way beyond the job description.

Cons

- Many people make the mistake of believing that simply going through the motions is enough.
- Most students are intimidated by the people they work under, so they avoid being assertive.
- Too many people waste a great opportunity because they are embarrassed to ask for help or advice.
- If you allow it, there is a chance you will become little more than the classic "gopher."

- If you achieve only what is asked of you, the internship can be a waste of your time.

- Too many students get lazy during internships or simply blow them off because they are not being paid.

Hey, it's your time, so make the most of it. Take advantage of the internship opportunity. Aside from completing the work you will be asked to do, push for the chance to go out with a reporter and learn how things happen "in the field." This is a major plus which will also open the door for you to get some work on tape. Ask for the opportunity to do a "stand-up" (the part of the story when you see a reporter on camera) when the person you are working with is done with his or her work.

Because getting work on tape is so vital to getting your first job, don't be afraid to pursue the opportunity to go out into the field with a reporter. What you do is save the tape with your "stand-up" on it, and when the reporter is done with the field tapes used for his or her story, you can write your own version. Once you've done this, you can schmooze an editor to help you put it together. Usually just being friendly and offering a dinner or lunch in exchange for his efforts can do the trick. But whatever it takes, maximize your internship experience by getting some stories on tape.

The reason we emphasize getting work on tape is because in the world of TV broadcasting, a paper resume only shows "where" you've worked and gained experience. While that's all well and good, the key to landing a job is your on-air work. And the only way to highlight that is on a tape. And the only way to have a tape is by reporting stories in the field. Get it?

We also know that you may have the opportunity to get a tape together of your work in some of your classes. We hope you will because that's more experience, meaning more practice at grooming your skills. However, if it comes down to having a chance to get some work on tape from a professional photographer at a TV station versus using video shot by you or some other student, you're almost always going to look better using the tape shot by a pro. Trust us, we both used to shoot our own video at one point, and we don't brag about the results.

All right, you've got the idea of how crucial an internship is. Now all you have to do is get one. There are a number of ways to attain an internship. You can apply with your advisor or the head of your communications or broadcasting department. Schools normally offer internship programs for which you'll receive credit hours. If your school doesn't offer course credit for internships, don't dump the idea. The main thing that counts is the experience, (and the tape you might get), so any class credit you receive will be a bonus.

At some schools, internships may only be offered to seniors. So if you are an underclassman, that would present a problem. In the case where your school does not offer a broadcasting internship program, don't let that stop you from getting one. Pick up a phone and contact a local station in your area. Introduce yourself, tell them about your aspirations, and ask about any internships they may offer. You will likely be able to get one rolling all by yourself, while at the same time make some great contacts in the business. Remember, once you get a reporting job, making these "cold" calls to strangers is similar to phone calls you'll have to make to track down stories.

And if after exhausting all avenues, you've found that not a single station in your area offers an internship program, there's still hope. Call someone that you have seen on the air and admire, and let them know that you like their work. Refer to a specific story or broadcast you may recall. It will score major points with that person. Even if the story wasn't good, maybe it was memorable and they will still love the fact you remembered it. We have yet to meet someone in this industry that doesn't enjoy a nice long, one-sided conversation on their absolute favorite subject: THEMSELVES.

From here you can discuss setting up a kind of "personal" one-on-one internship. You'll be amazed at how many people will be flattered to take someone under their wing and teach them their craft. It shows great initiative on your part and gives you a chance to work side by side with a pro, not to mention it develops a great relationship with someone in the business that can give you invaluable advice.

Internships are usually set up for students to place themselves in the actual working environment of a chosen profession. They are supposed to last one semester and provide the student with college credit for their services (and maybe a pat on the back). Most schools don't offer any credit past one semester, and very infrequently do the internships pay. If you can get a semester of credit, go for it. But it takes longer than one semester to gain the full advantages of an internship in a television newsroom.

The duties you will be asked to perform range from the tedious to the tantalizing. Internships may be set up in the news, weather or sports department, depending on which area you wish to pursue.

To give you a feel for what your actual job will be as an intern, we'll run down what your duties will be like in a news or sports department.

News Internships

After getting a brief crash course on the workings of a newsroom, you'll be asked to answer phones, make phone calls, log tapes, and help out in various ways the person to whom you've been assigned. Don't let the fact that some of what will be requested seems trivial. If you're aggressive and on the ball, you will become a major asset.

Your first duty of course is to be an asset to the reporter or anchor you're working with, **but it's up to you to take that extra step to get more out of the internship than what's required**. Don't stay locked in the station. After you've proven yourself in the newsroom, go out on story assignments with reporters. Learn the craft of writing, editing, producing and talking in front of a camera. Observe and pay close attention to everything that goes on around you. Pick the brains of some of the reporters who are established in the market. Find out what they have done to get where they are. Always remember that contacts mean everything in the broadcasting business and are great sources for job leads. Get to know as many people in as many positions as you possibly can, and make sure you stay in touch with them.

It's up to you to make things happen during your internship. Don't wait for a reporter, or shooter or producer to ask you to go along on a story. Get in the habit of seeing how it is done by the pros: how they initiate story ideas, the calls they make, how they handle interviews, stand-ups, live shots.

When you are on shoots and stories, regardless of whether you are in news or sports, again, ask if you can shoot your own stand-up for future stories that you could put on your resume tape. When you get this chance, preparation is the ultimate key because you don't want to waste anyone's time while they are working. And don't be shy or embarrassed about asking for advice and suggestions on what to say in your stand-up. The reporters have years of experience and can help you make what you're saying clear, concise and relevant. All this will not only give you valuable experience in front of the camera, but you'll begin compiling lots of material to choose from when it comes time to start assembling your all-important resume tape.

Sports Internships

One of the first duties expected of you is logging televised sporting events and various sports feeds subscribed to by the station. It involves watching the game for key plays, recording the times they happened, and keeping the on-air personnel informed of anything strange or unique that may have taken place. Many times three to four games are going on at the same time if it's a busy weekend, so it's a must to be able to think quickly, and concentrate on more than one thing at a time. The highlights you list and pass along play a major part in getting a sportscast on the air. Without the best pictures and details from each game, any show will suffer.

Take all your duties very seriously. Catching a key highlight or story can be the difference between a good show and a great one. The important thing is not to spend your internship simply logging games and nothing more. Do whatever you are assigned with ENTHUSIASM AND COMPETENCE, and then take it a step further. Show the people in the sports department that you are serious about what you are doing, you want to learn more, and you can handle larger tasks and more responsibility. When you are logging games, make suggestions of which highlights may be best to use. (We can't guarantee they will take your advice every time, but the more you nail the top ones, they more confidence they will show in you.) Provide concise shot sheets to the sports staff that are legible and easy to understand. If you show some drive you will find yourself doing some of the more glamorous things shortly. Show the sports staff that you can be a valuable asset to the team.

Believe us, we have worked in the biggest and smallest markets in the country, and one thing stations in every market have in common is they are short-handed. They can always use another hard-working, capable body. Any competent help that can be provided is not only appreciated, but embraced. Do not fail to understand how important it will be to show initiative.

Volunteer to work as many hours as you can handle. Set up your schedule so you are there during the busiest times, like weekends and Friday nights in smaller markets.

If you land an internship at a small market station, take every step to learn how to shoot and edit video. If you show the ability to pick up these skills, the stations will likely put your talents to work by having you shoot stories and possibly do some actual editing. All of this will be outstanding experience because these are skills you will likely need on your first job in TV.

Next dilemma: major market internships versus small market internships. Based on our experiences, we both strongly believe if it comes down to one or the other, small market internships often have bigger payoffs. Here's why:

- Many major markets have unions, which means interns are extremely limited in what they can and can't do.

- Small markets have much smaller staffs, meaning there is normally more work and responsibility for interns.

- Oftentimes, the atmosphere is much looser and friendlier in small markets, so reporters and anchors are likely to be more flexible with what they allow you to do.

- At some small markets, after a month or two of interning, you have a shot at doing some actual reporting for the station, especially when they are short-handed.

- Major markets normally keep intern's duties limited to things that don't help your on-air skills, such as running errands or logging tapes exclusively.

Once you have completed the internship at a station, you'll be faced with your next question: "What's next?" Well, don't think for a moment that one semester of interning is where you should end it. Make the most of relationships you've developed and find out about the possibilities of continuing on with the station. Work it out so you can stay on longer and continue to develop everything you've been learning. Again, you likely will not get any class credit for your additional efforts, but don't let that diminish how valuable any extra newsroom work can be. If you have your act together, you will become almost as valuable as a full-time employee and feel like part of the staff.

Believe it or not, there is a possibility if you extend your internship past its initial run, that you may actually have a chance to be paid for your work. We both have seen times where interns stay on and get on the payroll as associate producers. Another possibility is being hired on at your station after you graduate from college, but don't count on it.

By the end of your internship, you should have a couple of packages and a number of stand-ups on tape. In addition, it's always a major coup to get some anchoring experience. This can be done by talking with producers, reporters and anchors about the possibility of setting up a time when you can sit on the set and actually run through a broadcast or cut-in. The best time is immediately after an early newscast on the weekends (that's the least hectic and most realistic time to pull it off). You'll need to set this up through a producer who can keep the crew around following the early broadcast for your run-through. By doing this, it will allow you at the very least to do a segment of the broadcast that was just completed. When possible, write your own leads and story copy.

Along with strong writing and journalistic instincts, this business is also about personality, and yours is the one that needs to jump through that television screen. When you have interned at a station for an extended time, try to practice anchoring at least every month or so. It will require persistence, but you will notice unbelievable improvements.

And one final thing. Hang on to the copies of your first few stand-ups and early runs on the anchor set. This makes for great material to look back on as your career progresses. You'll get a kick out of seeing yourself on old tapes and be excited about how far you've come.

Internship
REVIEW

Learn all you can
about the television industry.

Go above and beyond
the call of duty.

Push
to get all the on-air experience
possible by writing stories, shooting
stand-ups and anchoring.

Accumulate
enough material so you can put together a
first-class and polished resume tape.

Putting Together a Winning Resume Tape

"Ambition, confidence, enthusiasm, and success
are produced by
courage, faith, pride and hard work."

H E N R Y   F O R D

In the world of television, your resume tape is far and away the most important element in landing or missing out on a job opportunity. Your video resume will be what you send out to stations all over the country, and will be the only way potential employers can judge your talent and on-air persona. We can't over emphasize just how critical it is for you to go to great lengths to make your resume tape as impressive, professional, and effective as possible.

Between the two of us, we have assembled, screened, and critiqued hundreds of tapes from people with various levels of experience from all over the country. We both studied tapes and got suggestions from numerous respected broadcasters as to what works on a tape and what doesn't.

One thing you need to realize right up front: because they get flooded with hundreds of tapes each and every month, IF A NEWS DIRECTOR IS NOT IMMEDIATELY IMPRESSED WITH WHAT THEY SEE ON A TAPE—THEY WILL NORMALLY

GIVE UP ON IT WITHIN THE FIRST 10–15 SECONDS. So with this imbedded firmly in your mind, you know right out of the box, not only are you competing against others for a job, you're also fighting against a news director's busy schedule.

We can promise you there is no "perfect" or "foolproof" way to put a resume tape together. It's a very subjective process, meaning that it's impossible to please each and every news director who will see your tape.

With this in mind, we believe through our collective years of experience, along with feedback from station managers, consultants, and other broadcasters, the following guidelines will help you put together a killer resume tape.

Length

For the most part, keep your resume tape fairly brief. Put the tape together with the idea that it needs to grab an individual's attention and have them begging to see more—usually, somewhere between three to seven minutes in length, depending on how much quality material you have to work with. Always make sure to limit your tape to what you believe is your best work. If it's borderline, don't use it.

Another point to keep in mind: make sure you appear on camera somewhere near the beginning of the tape. It makes no sense to start off with two minutes of video before you show yourself in a stand-up, live or anchoring situation. As you may already realize, **this is a business where appearance does count.** Whether that's fair or not is irrelevant, **IT'S A FACT**. So make sure to show anyone who is viewing your tape that you look well groomed and presentable, and more importantly, that you are relaxed and comfortable in front of the camera.

A good rule to remember about length: it's easy for a resume tape to be too long. Rarely is a tape considered too short. Try and leave everybody who views your tape wanting to see more, not feeling like they've seen too much.

Content

Next step: What do you put on your resume tape? Whether you have a lot of work to choose from or simply have a few stories, anchoring takes, and or live shots, put on your tape what makes you look and sound the best you possibly can. Do whatever you can to present a tape that is dynamic, informative, well edited, and one that will grab the attention of anyone who looks at it.

Pacing is a key element in any news broadcast, so you'll want to make sure your tape has good pacing. That means keep it moving. Don't allow any one segment to go too long, unless it's extremely strong video or a riveting interview you've done. Again we emphasize there's not necessarily any standard format to follow when putting together your tape. Your job is to find the right mix to present your work in the best possible way.

On most occasions the first job you will apply for is a reporter's position. So pieces that demonstrate your work in the field will likely carry most of the load. Tailor the tape to whatever position you're pursuing. If it's a straight news job, lead off with your best hard news and breaking stories. You can then follow it up with a lighter feature story that shows more of a creative style and personality. If you have some strong anchoring clips, make sure to include them as well. **You want to demonstrate and showcase all your abilities.** And if it's more of a feature or entertainment position your aiming for, then lead off the tape with stories fitting that description. The same goes for sports and weather positions. When it comes to sports, keep in mind that stations tend to look for personality driven tapes that include creativity and high energy.

If at all possible, showcase some animated cross talk with a co-anchor or guest. This is another opportunity for you to highlight your personality. Remember, you always want to present a dynamic, informative, well-edited tape that grabs the attention of everyone who views it.

As for separating your stories, live shots, and anchoring pieces, you need only a second or two of black between each item. Do not put individual countdowns between your elements. This way it keeps your stories separate, while not slowing down the pace of your tape.

Opening Montages

If you do have a substantial amount on tape to choose from, here's one idea we've found to be effective. Try starting out your tape with a montage, using quick bits of stand-ups, anchor takes, and lives shots combined back to back. Normally, use between four to eight different clips, running no longer than 30-45 seconds. Using a "montage open" allows a news director to see and hear you immediately and get a feel for what kind of on-air talent you are. By using a variety of different cuts in under a minute, you can display your on-air presence in a variety of settings and show off your diversity. We highly recommend this if you're trying to land a sports gig. Try experimenting with music under the montage as well (this can increase the pacing and keep the tape moving). But whenever you incorporate music into your tape, be sure it's enhancing, not distracting, and that it doesn't drown out what you're saying.

While a "montage open" is not a necessity, it serves a better purpose than putting on a story that runs over a minute before you and your face appear on the tape. Believe us, even if it's a strong story, news directors want to see you on camera as soon as possible. The rare exception would be a story that starts off so strong both visually and with sound that it will force someone to keep watching until you appear on camera.

Montage opens can be effective in various ways:

1. It's different. When a news director has the monumental task of viewing hundreds of tapes to fill one job, you must find a way to make yours stand out. One way to do that is with a clever and eye catching montage open. Make sure it looks and sounds memorable, but avoid making it seem too choppy.

2. A montage also shows you've taken an extra step to put together a strong piece. You are not simply content with slapping together a couple of reports or shows. Your creative open helps demonstrate you put in the extra effort to make your work stand out.

But while montage opens can prove to be effective for grabbing someone's attention, this is merely a "tease" to the real substance of your work on the tape. And as we told you earlier, no magic formulas exist for doing your resume tape. That means that while some people will enjoy a montage open, others will not be big fans and may strongly dislike them.

As for a slate at the head of the tape with your name and address, we don't believe it's necessary. It can be perceived as a waste of time by someone who's watching it if it runs too long. Besides, you should already have your name and address typed clearly on the outside of the tape and on the tape itself. You'll need to do this to make yourself easy to reach if your tape gets separated from your resume and cover letter. News directors normally have stacks of tapes in their offices, so **make sure your box is labeled on the side where your name will stand out**. Who knows, this could possibly make someone reach for your tape first.

Format

The tapes you send out should be on a 3/4-inch tape, unless another format is requested. There will be a few exceptions where you may have to put it on beta or super VHS, but 3/4-inch is a universal size nearly all stations use for resume tapes.

Always make sure to view any copies you make of your resume tape from start to finish. This allows you to ensure there are no problems on the tape and all the copies are clean.

Another minor key that can be a big help is enclosing a list of what items are included on your tape. For example:

1. Open stand-up and live shot montage

2. Fire rescue story

3. Feature Halloween story

4. Solid live report or anchoring segment

This allows anyone who gets the tape to easily peruse your work and know exactly what's on the tape. If possible, it's not a bad idea to put the running length of each segment next to the items along with a total tape time.

We shouldn't have to say this, but because some people don't understand, we will. **ALWAYS TYPE INFORMATION** you send along on a tape. This includes labels, index cards, resumes, and cover letters. Sloppy and unprofessional handwritten items reflect poorly on you as a possible job candidate. Develop good habits from the beginning.

You are looking for every edge over any potential competitors, and paying attention to small details is one way of getting that upper hand. It demonstrates you are thorough, organized, and committed to quality—all necessary traits of a successful broadcaster.

A few final tape tips. You have what you feel is a credible resume tape set to be sent all over the country. And now you're wondering, how do you go about getting tapes to make copies and what's the best way to do it?

One way is to go to a local television station, preferably one where you interned or have a few contacts. Check with the news director's secretary and others in the newsroom about extra tapes they have stacked up somewhere. Under most circumstances, they will be able to part with a handful of them and will be happy to get rid of some. Get as many as you can handle. You will need them. Remember, you're choosing one of the most competitive businesses in the world, so you'll need a high volume of tapes to send out.

Another reason it's imperative to stock up on tapes is this. When you apply for a job in a small market, you rarely get your resume tapes back. It's expensive and labor intensive for stations to return them all.

Dubbing Tapes

As for getting copies made of your master resume tape, we list a few options. One of the easiest and least expensive is going to your local cable access station or your college if you still live in that city. These outlets will probably have facilities to make dubs, so take time to find out where and when you can do it.

If that doesn't work, you can always try contacting the station you interned at or stations where you've made contacts. Normally for a small fee ($10–$50), you will be able to find a photographer, editor or a reporter at a small market who will help out. Make sure, though, not to take advantage of somebody's kindness.

Resume Tape
REVIEW

Keep the tape between three to seven minutes,
depending on how much quality material you have to offer. It's always better to leave them wanting more, rather than feeling they've seen too much.

No corny or cheesy opens.
If you want to show creativity, include a dynamic and appealing montage at the head of the tape. Remember to get your face on the screen at or near the top.

Customize your tapes if at all possible.
If you are applying for a job in news, gear you material towards news information. Same goes for sports, weather and entertainment.

Keep things moving on the tape.
Don't put a countdown between every story. Just a second or two of black works just fine and doesn't slow down the pacing. Start your tape with no more than a five-second countdown.

Make sure
your tape and the box you send are well labeled. Always type everything and include a list of individual items on the tape.

Writing an Effective Cover Letter

"Experience shows that
success is due less to ability than zeal.
The winner is he who gives himself to
his work, body and soul."

CHARLES BUXTON

So now you have a killer resume tape ready to be viewed by news directors across the country. The key now is to make sure you don't accompany it with a cover letter that is going to cost you the job before you even get it. We've both seen those infamous cover letters from hell. We will let you know right up front: **a cover letter won't get you a job in TV, but a sloppy and poorly put together letter could prevent you from getting one**.

The best thing about cover letters in broadcasting is simply that they make contact with a station where you're looking to land a job. But unlike most businesses, the cover letter holds limited water when it actually comes down to landing an on-air position. As we've pointed out, what will ultimately land you the gig is your resume tape showing YOU on camera.

A cover letter should basically express interest in a position and possibly offer a brief outline of your experience. Something simple and to the point, to let the news director or whomever is doing the hiring, know for which job you're applying. In some instances, you may simply explain you are sending a tape to get some kind of feedback on your work. Keep in mind as you write your cover letter, it's a nice introduction and, of course, you want to sound good, but it will not land you the job. The best thing you can hope for from your letter is to grab somebody's attention and get them to actually look at your tape.

The way we see it, our experience and discussions with news directors tells us cover letters need to be short and sweet. Don't get cute. And don't bother bragging or trying too hard to impress anybody. Get the important information down on paper, write it aggressively, and be energetic. Briefly describe what your background is, what your present situation is, and what you want from the station. Make sure to emphasize why you will be an asset to the station, but don't over-do it. Let them know you're young, hungry, and aggressive, not to mention excited about whatever opportunities lie ahead. And while you probably could go on about yourself forever, letting everyone know why you're perfect for the job, keep your cover letter to a **maximum of one page**. Save all the other information for when you actually go in for an interview.

A couple of final thoughts on writing a cover letter. Always make sure to **address it to a specific person**. "To whom it may concern" just doesn't cut it. And a letter addressed "Attention News Director" or anything close to these generic type of titles won't impress anyone either. Take the time and make the effort to find out exactly who it is you need to address your letter to and use their name. Call ahead and get the name and correct spelling of the news director or whomever it is you will be sending the tape. Don't rely on a broadcasting manual for names and address. Too many times people change jobs and titles, and if you don't call to check, you may get burned.

If at all possible, use a reference in the letter of someone you may know that will ring a bell or catch the reader's eye. For example, "I spoke with Joe Bag-Of-Donuts about your station, and he suggested I contact you." A familiar name is always a plus. Do not allow yourself to ever make the mistake of writing some standard cover letter to a station. **Make sure to personalize it every single time!**

Cover Letter

R E V I E W

Keep the cover letter
short and simple.
Don't let it exceed a maximum of one page.

Don't bother
trying to land the job through the letter.
You sell yourself with the tape.
The letter is merely your introduction.

Avoid
losing the job because of a tacky or
unprofessional letter.

Check and double check
to make sure there are no misspelled
names or words.

Always
address the cover letter to a specific person.
No generic titles allowed.

In Search of
that First Job

"Success is never final and failure never fatal.
It's courage that counts."

GEORGE F. TILTON

You've figured out by now that television news directors aren't hanging out on campuses or wandering the streets looking for someone to anchor their late newscast (or early newscast, or midday, or anything for that matter). To even be considered a candidate for a job, you must make contact with stations and get your tape circulating.

The first step you'll want to take after getting that killer resume tape and cover letter together is to pinpoint some markets to attack. There are some 200 television markets in this country; the smaller their number, the bigger the market. For example, New York is the number one market in the country. Number two is Los Angeles, number three is Chicago, etc. When you launch your job search, be realistic.

The best way to groom yourself for a successful career is by becoming a good on-air reporter or anchor. And the only way to become a solid on-air talent is getting a job and **doing it every day**. The most likely place you'll be able to get a full-time, on-air job, right out of school with little or no real experi-ence, is in a smaller market.

We both have heard college students and others tell us they want to break into the TV business, but they don't want to spend any time honing their skills in a small market. They say they grew up in a big city, have always lived in a big city, and they insist on landing a reporting job in a major market imme-diately. Rather than getting an on-air job in a small market re-porting and learning all that goes along with being a reporter or anchor by doing it every day, we hear from people who say they would prefer taking a job at the assignment desk or as a writer in a big market instead.

Any time we get a call or meet someone with this attitude, we tell them, "If you're serious about becoming a reporter and/ or an anchor, get over the arrogant and ridiculous attitude." It makes no difference if you grew up in New York City or Donut Hole, Montana; if you want to master your on-air skills at the fastest rate possible, the only way to do it is to actually do it. In other words, by reporting every day in a smaller market, you'll develop into a solid reporter long before you could ever dream of becoming a skilled on-air talent by simply sitting at an as-signment desk, being a production assistant, or doing a job as some kind of gopher in a major market.

For those who still aren't convinced reporting and anchor-ing in a small market beats any other "off-air" job at a major market, think about it this way: if a news director has a reporter position open, who do you think they would consider a better candidate? A person who spent two years at an assignment desk in a big market, who had no on-air experience, or a person who spent two years out in the field reporting in a small mar-ket, breaking stories, covering live events, and doing this five days a week, every week for two years? Clearly, it's no contest. You didn't learn to ride a bike by watching all the other kids in the neighborhood cruise by your house on two wheels every-day, now did you?

The next step is finding out about job openings and getting your tape in front of the right people.

There are a number of different ways to go about this. One way is simply by hustling your tape around various small markets. This can be done by mail or in person. If at all possible, doing it live and in living color is normally your best option. This allows you to meet with the prospective employers face to face and it also gives you a chance to let all your natural charisma come out (just like on that hot resume tape). The best way to set up a meeting at a station is to call ahead and make contact with the news director. Many times, news directors won't immediately take phone calls from strangers. Some are simply too busy, while others just like acting like they never have time for anyone who phones in. And even though some of them are spending much of their busy day playing video golf on their computers, news directors will normally be tough to contact personally.

While you sit there wondering how to get through to these video game playing people who run newsrooms, realize there is no sure fire way to pull it off. But we do have a few suggestions. One way to attack it is by making contact with somebody else in the newsroom first. A reporter, someone on the assignment desk, or even a secretary that sounds friendly when you call. Many times, these people are great contacts and become good allies when trying to get in to speak with a news director. At the very least, if you still have trouble lining up a meeting with the person that heads up the station, give your tape to whom you've made contact with and have them pass it along to the person in charge. That way if they're interested, they have the opportunity to take a break from their busy day to call you.

If you are able to get through on the phone to a news director, work the conversation toward meeting face to face. Let them know you'd like to come in at their convenience to discuss your tape and talk over possible job opportunities. This will open the door for you to prove to this individual that you'll be someone worth having on board. And don't let a quick "We have no jobs open at this time" stop your pursuit. Even if there are no present openings, let the news director know you'd simply like to meet for some feedback on your tape and have the opportunity to watch a newsroom in action. That way when an opening does occur, you have an immediate advantage.

Before we move on, there is one thing we must make loud and clear when dealing with news directors. **DON'T BE A PEST, OR YOU ARE LIKELY TO BE EXTERMI-NATED.** Seriously, they are very busy people with more things on their minds than simply making one hiring decision. When you call them, be smart.

Only contact a news director during a time that doesn't interfere with daily newscasts. In smaller markets, the news director may be a producer or anchor, so no phone calls after 3 p.m. The best time to reach most of them is after their morning meetings, somewhere between 10:00 a.m. and 1:00 p.m.

Now, for some other ways to get your tape flowing in front of the faces of the right people in the right places, there are several options. A number of consulting firms exist to help in the area of showing off your tape. A couple of examples are The Frank Magid Group and Don Fitzpatrick and Associates. These two firms are among many which work closely with stations all over the country. By getting your tape out to companies such as these, your work will be seen by a large volume of people, which in turn enhances your odds of being "discovered." But do be advised, this should just be one small part of your job pursuit.

With your resume tape in hand, there are a number of ways to check out the "grapevine" for job openings. The following is a list of ways to keep up on what's going on in the field of broadcasting and what jobs may be available:

1. A phone service called Media Line. This is a service that charges a monthly fee and has "on-air" job listings in the field of TV and radio broadcasting recorded daily on a message line. It gives out information on some select openings, and records them separately into the categories of news, sports or weather.

   The recorded messages normally include the specific position, what station it's at, the kind of experience the applicant should have (don't let that get in the way; remember, if someone likes your work, that may be enough to get an interview), and the name and address of the person to whom you should send your tape and cover letter. Oftentimes, the recorded message concerning a job will say "no phone calls."

   While we don't suggest you call and bother someone, we do strongly recommend you at least make a follow-up call to the person you sent the tape to about a week or so after you send. This is a good way to make sure they got the tape, and gives you a chance to get some feedback.

2. The Pipe Line. Same idea as Media Line, different name.

3. Many publications such as *Broadcasting* magazine and *Electronic Media* print job openings. They list all the important information you'll need on select opportunities. (While these first three items can lead to solid job openings, they sometimes may be outdated and already filled by the time you read or hear of them.

4. Attend broadcasting conventions that go on throughout the year in different cities. RTNDA (Radio & Television News Directors Association) and the NABJ (National Association of Black Journalists) are just two examples. Groups like these hold at least one annual meeting across the country and oftentimes include job fairs, informational meetings, and are great ways to meet people in the business who may help you get where you want to be.

5. Word of mouth remains one of the most effective ways to hunt down a TV or radio gig. Speak with people in the business, university instructors, and consulting firms.

In Search of that First Job
REVIEW

Have a carefully thought-out list
of realistic markets in which you want to work.
Include geographic preferences and market
size into your equation.

Get to know
the names of the influential people who will do
the hiring at these stations.

Keep them updated
with current work of yours. Make it a point to
correspond with them by letter and phone on a
fairly regular basis.

Work to establish
and nurture contacts within different
newsrooms. These people can become great
allies to learn from and be helpful in
tracking down job leads.

Look into
subscribing to a service that informs clients
where job openings are.

Agents:
The Good, The Bad,
The Ugly

"Success is a journey — not a destination."

H. TOM COLLARD

We can't explain it, but someone, somewhere put the word out that signing with an agent or agency is the miracle answer to getting that first gig in television. For the record, let us set one thing straight: **an agent merely creates an opportunity or opens the door, YOU and YOUR TALENT get the job and keep it.**

In the early stages of the job search, don't get caught up in the idea that you need an agent to break in. The reality is, you do not need an agent to get your first "on-air" job, and when it comes right down to it, we recommend not even wasting your time with an agent until you have begun a career reporting or anchoring. The reasons we believe dealing with an agent in the early stages of your career is a waste of your time are clear and simple:

1. Most quality agents and agencies won't even bother trying to sign you until you have some experience

and show you have some real potential in the television business. In other words, it's a waste of *their* time to deal with someone with little or no work experience.

2. Any legitimate agent that believes in you would be more likely to give you advice to help you along and act as a bit of a "mentor" in the early going, with the ultimate hope of you turning into a solid talent, giving the agent a great chance of representing you when you are truly ready and in need of representation.

3. Understand there are plenty of shady agents and agencies out there who have little desire to work hard to do what's best for you. They're simply interested in getting you any job that pays money, so they can make a few bucks off of you.

4. The reality is, you won't be making much money in the beginning, so most top rate agents wouldn't work for you to get paid a small percentage of the already small salary you'll make in that first job. On the other side of that, even if 10% of your salary seems small, you don't want to be coughing it up in your first couple of jobs, because if you're only making peanuts to begin with, you'll need to keep them all.

5. And the major reason why you don't need to bother with an agent before you get your first job, or your second or third one for that matter, is that you can do an adequate job of selling and showing off your skills in the beginning. Besides, most small and many medium size markets refuse to deal with agents. (And normally, smaller markets don't have to deal with agents because the majority of their on-air talent don't have them.)

The main role of an agent is to negotiate contracts, provide you with critiquing and coaching sessions that will enhance your skills, seek out and discover new opportunities, and represent you in any problems that may flare up in the newsroom.

Normally you won't need an agent until your career begins breaking into the top 15-25 markets. You may run into several agents or agencies who say **"you've got what it takes"** after only knowing you a short while and promise "they know all the top news directors and general managers at all the best stations." Beware of this type of overzealous agent who does a lot of double talk and pushes to get your name on a contract. Use some common sense. Most of these types are out for a quick buck. They realize if they get a high enough volume of clients, especially those in small markets or just breaking in who don't know any better, the opportunity is there for them to make money off of "quantity" rather than "quality."

Bottom line: **don't even sweat the idea of an agent when you first get out of school and you're trying to nail down that first job.** Use your time and energy putting together a hot tape, start sending them out, and get out into the field and start pushing your talents on your own. **Be your own agent**. Nobody believes in you more than you. Nobody is willing to work harder for you than you. And when you're not making a ton of money, who would you rather pay 10% at the end of the month than you? NOBODY.

Because we don't want to offend all agents on the planet, let us point out there are some very good ones out there who do truly take an interest in you as a person and can be good for your career. We are represented by two of them. In the same breath, we both agree agents are a "necessary evil" at some point in most careers. Again, to avoid alienating every agent who practices the art of selling and negotiating, we only use the word "evil" because any time you sign a contract to give away your hard-earned dollars, you have to admit that's an evil feeling. But an agent who sincerely has more in mind than just squeezing you for a fist full of dollars (trust us, there are a few quality ones floating around) can be helpful in both getting a good job, and possibly make that good job better and more lucrative.

Some advice for down the road. After you're past your first couple of jobs and in line to start making some serious cash, think long and hard about having an agent represent you and **do your homework**. The person you ultimately hire to work for you must be an individual you feel good about, believe in and trust. Get to know the person, interview the prospective agents over an extended period of time, and find out others they represent and interview them. Also, go beyond talking to clients that an agent may suggest you talk with, because unless the agent is a total idiot, any client they suggest you talk to will only sing their praises. Look for other people to interview about a particular agent, even one or two clients who may have dumped the agent. This will allow you to get all the good, the bad, and the ugly information on the individual agent.

Once you've established a relationship with an agent you feel is on the same page, make that individual prove to you why it's worth giving them a part of your monthly income.

A few questions you may want to ask

- Why should I invest my money in you?
- Why do you want to represent me?
- Because I won't be your only client, how will I know you'll always be available when I need you?
- What if I decide before the contract is up that it's not working out?
- What kind of work will you be doing for me after you place me in a new job or better position?
- What other services does your agency provide besides negotiating contracts and setting up job interviews?
- How can you prove to me you can negotiate a contract above and beyond what I could do?

Another thing to definitely consider about an agent is how many other clients they represent who are similar to you (gender, experience, and area of expertise), and what size markets those individuals are in. Here's why this factor is so important. Say you have a job in the 55th market. You're a sportscaster looking at an opening in Kansas City, which is the 29th market. You know there will be some healthy competition for that position, so one of the last things you want to do is battle someone who is represented by your own agent. It happens all the time. They may represent a handful of clients similar to you in many ways, and when there is an opening, they will submit ALL of you for the same job. When a situation like this occurs, there is no way agents can possibly represent you fairly or to the fullest, because they will be campaigning two or more individuals for one opening. So in the end, agents will be the only ones who benefit from this type of scenario. While their chances increase for landing the job for a client, your percentages go down.

Some final thoughts on agents: This is one of the major decisions you will make in your career, and it should not be made in haste. Talk to some people who are represented by the agent you are considering. Find out what their strengths and weaknesses are. See what kind of results they've produced.

Always keep in mind, **agents work for you, not the other way around. You're the boss.** It's your career. While they can do the dirty work and give guidance, final decisions are up to you. You always call the shots.

Agents
R E V I E W

Don't rush into getting an agent.
Wait until you are at a point in your career
when they will legitimately help you.

Learn all you can
about an agency or agents in which you're
interested. Find out the services they provide,
other clients they represent, and how they
have helped further their careers.

**Don't count on an agent to do
all the work.**
Keep looking for jobs on your own and work in
conjunction with the agent you may hire.

Preparing for a Knockout Job Interview

"The road to success is usually off the beaten path."

FRANK TYGER

No doubt getting to the point of a job interview in television broadcasting may have completely tapped you out of energy, but your work is far from over. Yes, you need to reach an interview to ultimately get the job, but you must also realize how important the actual interview really is. Many people mistakenly dismiss it as a mere formality before getting the official offer. Don't fall into this line of thinking.

You may take a brief moment to pat yourself on the back for landing that job interview, but make it short and sweet, so you can get geared up for the next vital step. **Interviewing is a skill, just like what you do on your tape**. You need to be prepared and well-studied for the interview, similar to the way you would do background for a story you would cover.

Make sure to investigate some background and history of the station, and find out something about the person who will be conducting the interview. This allows you not only to sound educated with your responses and able to relate your answers directly to the station, but it also gets you prepared to ask some key questions regarding the market in general and the station specifically.

The number one mistake people make in the interview process is they simply go in and answer all the questions thrown their way. Most of these misguided souls think if they do an adequate job responding to everything asked during the conversation, that's enough to get the gig. Sounds good, but it's not that simple.

Most of the time, the person conducting the interview, normally the news director, will take control of the interview and ask a list of questions. Some do it very formally and stick to a specific list of questions. Others will hold more of a conversation with you to keep it relaxed. Either way, when done, they will often ask, "Do you have any questions for me?" Don't ever respond like this: "No, not really, I can't think of any questions, I think you covered everything."

You need to realize while the station is interviewing you, you must be prepared to interview them as well. This is not only for your benefit, but it also lets whomever is running the interview know you care enough to ask educated questions and put the time in to prepare.

The more you know about a station and it's market, the better off you will be during the interview. You need to have your guns loaded with more than, "I'm a very hard worker and get along well with other people." Sounds silly, but you'd be amazed at how many people don't prepare themselves properly for an interview, become nervous during the process, and end up sounding like they aren't sure what their own name is. (Name tags are not the answer to that dilemma, by the way.)

Know where each station in the market rates, who the key talent is in the shop, the market trends, and any and all topical information that would be going on in that city or region. This will let you showcase your knowledge and reporting duties during the interview. And by having a good arsenal of responses, you will be able to elaborate on topics and be able to answer things in a confident and successful manner.

You must also take the opportunity to be aggressive enough during the interview to speak up and ask questions from time to time. You need not wait until you are asked if you have any.

While you want to avoid sounding at all rude, it never hurts to be aggressive enough to speak up and inject opinions on topics and ask some of your own questions throughout.

We serve up a list of key questions **you** may want to ask during an interview:

- **Describe to me the qualities that make up your best/ideal reporter? Anchor?** A question like this early in the interview is key for several reasons. By listening closely to the response (maybe even jotting down some notes) you will soak up valuable information that will help you answer later questions. You will hear first hand what this person looks for and expects from a reporter/anchor and you will be able to explain throughout the conversation in subtle ways why you fit those characteristics.

- **What is your newsroom philosophy?** This is key because you will get a good idea where they are coming from and how they like to cover and present the news.

- **What convinced you to get into the business?** This gives you a good background of their motivation. Another good thing to feed off of as you respond to questions.

- **What are your goals and plans for this station?** This is a good way to discover their long range objectives. By investigating this, you'll have a better feel on how you may fit into their plans, and whether they fit into yours.

- **What do you like about television in this market and what changes are needed to take it to the next level?** Another good question for some background on what this person expects.

- **What did you see on my tape that convinced you to interview me for the job?** By asking this, you will get a feel for what they think of your current work and what kind of potential they feel you have.

Now, to state the obvious about your job interview. **LOOK GOOD. LOOK SHARP. DRESS PROFESSIONALLY.** Fair or not, we are judged everyday of our lives by our appearance. Don't make the mistake of creating any negative first impressions when you're going into a station to have that initial face to face with a prospective employer.

The likely reality is you don't have a closet full of Hugo Boss suits or dresses by Giorgio Armani. If you do, throw on your favorite and knock 'em dead. But it's the person in the clothes, not the one who made them, who is going to get the job. Because you have control over what you wear, be selective. Nothing too loud or flashy. Go more for understated elegance. If you feel comfortable with clothes, and you think you understand fashion, then you are set. But for the fashion impaired, don't take your job interview attire lightly. Your appearance will play some part in the process.

Make sure you find your best look. For women, a classic looking dress, skirt or suit is a good start. Men should go with a suit and tie. If you are interviewing for a job at MTV, BET, or VH-1, there's a chance "casual-cool" will be accepted, maybe even expected. If there is any doubt or question, make life easy. Call the interviewer you're meeting with and ask.

Knockout Job Interview
R E V I E W

Prepare for the interview.
Be ready for anything they might throw at you.

Be proactive, not reactive.
Have a list of intelligent and relevant questions prepared. Show the interviewer that not only do you want the job, you are the best person for it.

Investigate
the station, the key players in the interview and the entire market. Know who wins the ratings war.

Look sharp.
Be confident. Get the job. Then celebrate like crazy.

Tube Tips

"Keep your eyes on the stars and your feet on the ground."

THEODORE ROOSEVELT

If you are like us, and we wouldn't wish that on anyone, but if you are, then working in television is something you've wanted to do and planned for a very long time. Once you get that first job, it's going to seem almost unbelievable for a short time. Then you'll see your first pay check, and you won't want to believe it. (Because it's so small.) Seriously, we hope your main motivation to get in this business was not to get rich quick. Yes, the opportunities to make a very good living increase the further along you progress. And when you get to the best jobs in the biggest markets, your compensation will be spectacular. But you can't enter such a subjective business solely because someday, through a lot of hard work, sacrifice and luck, the potential is there to make a tremendous amount of money.

We hope you decided to pursue a job in this profession, because like us, it's **IN YOUR BLOOD**. You not only enjoy the pressure of daily deadlines, but you thrive on it. You live for the pursuit of an important, compelling and entertaining story.

But just like any other profession, there are ups and downs, pros and cons, bump and runs, pick and rolls, advantages and disadvantages. The more you know entering the field, the better off and more prepared for success you will be.

Television broadcasting is without question one of the most subjective businesses in the world. Think about it. If you are a doctor or lawyer, it's easy to determine who the best are—the ones that have successful surgery backgrounds, are experts in diagnoses, or proven winners in litigation, etc. In television, you present yourself to the public, and they are the ones who will make the decision whether or not to like you.

Sometimes people choose to dislike a television personality for the most trivial reasons. They may not like your hair, the way you pronounce a certain word, the amount of makeup you wear, your clothes, your smile (your pierced tongue, yellow teeth or four chins). Realize that going in.

Work hard to make yourself presentable and professional, but no matter what you do, it won't be good enough for some people. That's why it's so important to **BE YOURSELF**. Develop a style that is comfortable for you, and don't deviate. Don't reinvent yourself. Don't try to be someone else.

The public can sniff out a phony in no time. If you always remember to be yourself on the air, it is much easier to accept any negative criticism you may receive from viewers and media critics. If they don't like you, too bad. But do keep an open mind to any constructive criticism from people you know and whose opinions you respect. No matter what stage you are at in your career, there is always room for improvement. Be professional. The people that have the longest, most successful careers are the ones that always look for ways to improve, yet stick to a style they feel comfortable with that reflects the type of person they are.

Tube Tips
REVIEW

Work hard.
Have a great attitude. Be confident, yet humble. Remember the qualities you possess that got you to this point.

Be aware
of other opportunities available in the marketplace. You don't always have to send tapes out, but be aware, because there are forces you can't control in this business, that you should always be prepared for the unexpected.

Never
forget there's always more to learn in this business. No matter where you may work, there is someone out there, oftentimes a colleague, with more experience, talent and ambition. Learn from these individuals, and continue to grow and improve.

Invest in a 401 (k).
Put some money in savings. And call your parents once in a while. You wouldn't be here without them.

Make Your
Next Move When It
Makes Sense

"Success is getting what you want.
Happiness is wanting what you get."

DAVE GARDNER

Guess what? Even though you will be thrilled to start your career in any market (most likely a small one), at some point you will be ready for a bigger challenge. (And bigger paycheck.) That may be after five years, three years, one year, six months, or as in our case, about 60 days.

Nothing against Sioux City, Iowa or Yuma, Arizona, but when you get delayed covering a high school girls softball game or library board meeting because you were stuck in traffic (behind a manure spreader), it may be time to update that resume. If the big news story of the year is how the local school board decided to switch from whole wheat to rye bread in the cafeteria, well, it may be time to move on.

More than likely, you won't be asked to sign a contract on your first job. Especially if it is in a market sized 100 or above. There is really no point locking yourself in for two or more years when you might outgrow the market in half that time.

We certainly don't recommend looking around until you

put in at least one year at your first job. There is just so much to learn, even though you may think you are prepared for the network after a couple of weeks. One of the most dangerous things you can do is get to a job that you aren't ready for, and end up getting fired. You will be back to square one.

We have both seen many resume tapes of people that were quite impressive, but when we called and asked the candidate for another sample of their work, we were very underwhelmed to say the least. So get the max out of every job. Understand what your weaknesses may be, and work to improve them.

Constantly look for outsiders' opinions. You can get valuable input from people both inside the business and out of it. Take for instance your family (you all have one of those) and friends (we hope you have a couple of those, too). It's always helpful and fun to watch their reaction when they see your work on TV. Do they seem compelled, interested, entertained, enthralled? Let's hope. A bad sign is if they doze off, keep looking at their watch, or if drool begins to form at the side of their mouth. That would mean they are bored out of their minds, and it's not the reaction that builds confidence.

People outside the business can always give you great input as to how your makeup, hair, clothes and overall appearance look on television. They are also usually pretty honest. Those are opinions that you need to hear. Most of the time they can see things that you miss. Like that old-fashioned haircut that you think looks sweet. Or that wide, knit tie that you haven't worn since Junior High School.

The bottom line is this. For the most part, we each tend to look for our good stuff in every story and every tape. We know how long and hard we worked on stories, and we want them to be good. But the important thing is to gauge how your audience of friends and family reacted. They are typical viewers. They can help you see what works and what doesn't. You can then apply this new knowledge when you get back to work.

Seek out Opinions from Experts

Don't be afraid to call people in the business that you respect or admire. Ask if you can send them a sample of your work for their review. Granted, some of these people may never call you back. They are either too busy, arrogant or uninterested to respond. Don't let it faze you.

The ones that do respond, however, may not send out lengthy letters, but just a note from them can provide the encouragement needed to overcome some hard times. Every successful person in television broadcasting has had his or her share of hardships and will understand exactly what you are going through. The cool ones are the people that respond, try to help, and offer advice and guidance.

(By the way: don't bother calling or writing the authors of this book for advice or suggestions. They are a couple of the arrogant ones mentioned earlier. JUST KIDDING! Actually, feel free to contact us for critiquing or advice.)

Make Your Next Move
When It Makes Sense

REVIEW

Make sure

you are ready for the next challenge
before you pursue it.

Try to spend a year

at your first job and learn all you can.

Get opinions

of your work from people you know.

Have people you admire

in the field critique your work.

Don't Be Dejected When You Get Rejected

"To be successful, you've got to be willing to fail."

FRANK TYGER

It's a little know fact that aggressive young television journalists are responsible for the destruction of about two million trees. Big ones. No, they don't moonlight as lumberjacks and haven't started any forest fires (as far as we know anyway). They simply have enough rejection letters in their files to circle the globe about six and a half times.

There's a good chance you will be turned down by some of the best and worst television stations in the country. As most of you already know, or will soon find out, nothing is more frustrating than not getting a job you feel you deserve.

The only thing that exceeds that level of frustration is losing out to someone you believe is less talented and qualified than you. It hurts! It's not fair! But it's also important for you to realize that this is a very realistic aspect of television broadcasting. You will be in that situation at some point in your career. The way you handle it may determine how successful you actually become.

Use the rejection as a wake-up call. There is a reason you didn't get the job, and usually it isn't obvious to you. When this happens, have someone in the business you respect take a long hard look at your resume tape. Allow their critical eye to help you decide if it is the best possible representation of your talents. If it appears it isn't, update the tape. Make the necessary changes to assure that the next time you send it out, the response is much more favorable.

When you fail to land the job you apply for, remember something we emphasized earlier: this is one of the most subjective professions on the planet. Whenever you get rejected for a position, it does not always reflect directly on your talents and skills. Oftentimes, only two or three people are involved in the selection process, so there's a good chance you simply didn't fit exactly what they were looking for. **Don't take it personally. Do find ways to improve your talents and tape.**

Don't Be Dejected When You Get Rejected

REVIEW

Remember

that everyone loses out on jobs they want at
some point in their career.

Figure out

what prevented you from getting that job
and improve.

Stay motivated

and work on your weaknesses so
the next time you send your tape out you get
the job you want.

The Wonderful World of Broadcasting: Myth vs. Fact

*"A successful person is one
who can lay a firm foundation with the bricks
that others throw at them."*

SIDNEY GREENBERG

Myth

You **MUST** stay at your first job at least a minimum of two years to develop a solid base before moving on to a bigger market.

Fact

Your first job will more than likely be at a small market, but there are no rules as to how long you should stay there. People will often tell you otherwise, but ultimately that decision will be decided by you and your station. If you want to stay there for 20 years, or want to move on after four and a half months, **YOU** need to make that decision. Be realistic in your goals and in evaluating your own talent and progress. Because it's an unpredictable business, do what feels right for you, and make sure whatever decisions you make keep you moving up the ladder.

Myth

Everybody in the world of television broadcasting makes big bucks.

Fact

Yes, a very small percentage of network and big market stars pull down salaries that professional athletes and movie stars would envy, but the odds of attaining that type of money are not in your favor. In reality, starting salaries in television news are some of the **LOWEST** of any profession. However, in this business you have the opportunity to double or triple your salary overnight.

If you have a fair amount of talent and an inordinate amount of drive and determination, you will make a very comfortable living in this business. And who knows, you might be one of the lucky ones pulling down seven figures.

Myth

The people who work the hardest, hustle, and break the big stories will always be rewarded with appropriate promotions.

Fact

Once again, there are no rules, especially when it comes to this particular subject. Television is a subjective business. Decisions made by station management will normally be based on opinion and not facts. What makes a good reporter depends on whom you are talking to at that particular moment. Don't get discouraged when you feel like you were overlooked for a promotion. Likewise, don't get too full of yourself when you get one. Your best approach will always be "control what you have control over." Do whatever you can to make yourself the best reporter or anchor you can possibly be.

CHAPTER
11

The Wonderful World of Broadcasting: Myth vs. Fact

Myth

You need to "sound" like a broadcaster to be a broadcaster.

Fact

Forget the stereotype. Don't try to sound like "Joe Broadcaster" or "Rhonda Reporter." Anyone who tries to turn on that broadcast voice will sound contrived and phony. You will always sound your best when you sound like you. **Keep it natural, real and conversational**. Speak in your normal voice and pacing. Don't try to sound like someone else. Figure out what makes you a unique individual and work to get to the point where you are comfortable enough to let that come out on the air. It's a highly competitive business and you need to do all you can to set yourself apart from the crowd.

Myth

The bigger the television market, the better the station.

Fact

While most people in bigger markets make more money, bigger markets do not always translate into higher quality television. Many times you will find medium size markets put more emphasis on quality in areas like video and production. Big city stations normally have more breaking news, so most of the time the focus is on the quantity of news stories, not necessarily the high-end production value you may see in other markets. If you aspire to work in the bigger markets, don't let the "slap and paste" attitude force you to accept it. Always keep your standards of excellence at a high level no matter what the attitudes are of your coworkers.

Myth

Anyone working in a big market must be one of the best broadcasters in the business.

Fact

While it is true that in most cases the cream does rise to the top, where a person works does not indicate the talent he or she may possess. Yes, some of the best reporters and anchors in the country are at top five markets or on the network level, but it certainly doesn't mean that smaller markets don't have extremely talented broadcasters. Some people with big league talent simply prefer to stay in smaller cities. And yes, some people working in the most desirable markets may have attained these positions for reasons other than talent and desire.

Myth

Unless you know someone, or just get a lucky break, you may never make it in this business.

Fact

The reality is, luck and having some well-placed contacts in this business are keys. But what many people fail to realize is you can **MAKE YOUR OWN BREAKS**. You must make yourself lucky. Create situations where you can put yourself in position to have things fall your way. That happens through hard work, and having a plan for your career. Make the extra efforts needed to set yourself apart from the competition. Strive to make all the breaks you dream of become reality. You'll figure out at some point that the people who constantly appear to get the lucky breaks are the people who work the hardest. The ones who make all the hard work look easy are the ones who have busted their butts for years to make it all seem so effort-

CHAPTER
11

The Wonderful World of Broadcasting: Myth vs. Fact

less. Some say it's better to be lucky than good. Maybe. Keep in mind, luck normally doesn't just happen by chance. **You have to give yourself every edge so you can be "luckier" than everyone else.**

The Wonderful World of
Broadcasting: Myth vs. Fact
R E V I E W

Not everyone
in the world of television broadcasting
makes big bucks.

The hardest working
broadcasters are not always rewarded. It's your
hard work and talents that create the big break.

You don't need
to have a stereotypical "broadcaster"
voice to be successful. Be conversational and
sound like yourself.

The market size
of a station doesn't always relate directly
to it's quality.

Final Thoughts

FROM TOM AND JON

The reality about the television business is there's no textbook approach to getting in, or magic formula to an illustrious career. (If there was, we'd be writing that book instead, and selling it for a couple hundred dollars.)

Simply put, you need to do all you can to make the most of whatever your God-given abilities may be. Make it a point to go the extra mile to set yourself apart from the crowd. Always keep in mind how many other people will be fighting for the same jobs and how **FEW** the opportunities actually are.

Concentrate on your writing skills, learn to be a great story-teller, focus on becoming a compelling and strong journalist. Take public speaking courses and speech classes so you can develop a comfortable presence. Prepare yourself as thoroughly as possible, so when you are in front of a camera doing your thing, whoever is watching will see **YOU**—the natural and real you.

While you can learn from professionals you admire and respect, don't bother trying to copy what they do. Don't force a style that doesn't fit your personality. As a matter of fact, don't even worry too much about style when you first break in. Work on all the basics, the fundamentals of becoming a solid reporter and anchor. You will find that gradually you will develop your very own, personalized style. As you become more relaxed on the air, your style will come out when your true personality works its way into your delivery.

Along with getting your act together as far as "on-air" skills, take full advantage of every opportunity out there to get that **"killer"** resume tape together. Intern, shadow a reporter or anchor you get to know, practice reading out loud, and look for interesting and creative ways to talk about what's going on in the world. It's not a scientific method that can be broken down, but understand this, the two of us have gone down the road a few miles and we've seen and studied what works. At the same time, we can tell you what won't get you very far—expecting some great television job to simply fall in your lap. And once you do land that first gig, keep your drive and motivation at a maximum level. By continually pushing to take your talents to the next level, you will forever force yourself to find new and innovative ways to communicate.

You are about to enter one of the most exciting, competitive, challenging and thoroughly rewarding careers that exists. It can also be a frustrating pursuit at times, as well as difficult and unfair. There are no free rides in this business. (OK, there are a few, but not many.) Approach it like Dennis Rodman attacks a hair salon or tattoo parlor. Be aggressive, have a plan, and do what is necessary to achieve your goals. (Without breaking the law or getting sued.)

The habits and work ethic you develop early in your career will stay with you throughout, and this is what will separate you from the pack of "wannabes" and "has beens" in the industry. The sky is the limit for you if you are willing to work, and continue to learn and grow. Remember, if you truly believe the television industry is for you, it's a wide open canvas, there are no set "rules" to the game, and as far as getting, keeping, and advancing to a better job, always **focus your energy on what you have control over—YOU AND YOUR TALENTS.**

Before we turn you loose, we truly wish you well in your quest for a career in this crazy and exhilarating world of television broadcasting.

Your journey has only just begun. We hope you have picked up many tips and suggestions from this book that will propel you to superstardom. Cheers to a bright, successful and satisfying future.

SPECIAL THANKS TO

RONALD MCDONALD HOUSE CHARITIES

LINDA SCHWARTZ PHOTOGRAPHY
CHICAGO

GRAPHIC ARTS STUDIO
BARRINGTON, IL

MULLIGAN PLUS MULLIGAN DESIGN
CHICAGO

NBC 5 TELEVISION
CHICAGO

INTERNET PRESENCE COORDINATORS
SCHAUMBURG, IL

KASTERZ MARKETING
CHICAGO

NOTES

NOTES

About The Authors:

Tom Zenner and Jon Kelley are sports anchors at NBC 5 Television in Chicago, Illinois. Prior to working together in Chicago they paid their dues at smaller stations around the country. Both received scholarships to play college football at the Division I level and graduated with degrees in Communications/Broadcasting.

Tom graduated from the University of Pacific, in Stockton, California in 1990. Before that he attended Normandale Junior College in Bloomington, Minnesota. During his two years there he broke O.J. Simpson's all time Junior College touchdown record with 56 career touchdowns. That record still stands. The Belgrade, Minnesota native served as Sports Director at KNXV Television, the ABC affiliate in Phoenix, Arizona before moving to Chicago in 1995.

Originally from Lincoln, Nebraska, Jon graduated from the University of Nebraska in 1988, and signed as a free agent with the Denver Broncos. He has worked in Chicago since 1991, and was promoted to Sports Director in 1995. Prior to working in Chicago, Jon was the weekend anchor at WDAF Television in Kansas City, Missouri.

Ironically, both Tom and Jon began their broadcasting careers at different stations in Sioux City, Iowa. From there, they both made stops in Omaha, Nebraska. Tom served as Sports Director at KPTM Television and KKAR Radio, while Jon was a news reporter at KMTV.

Together they have covered the biggest names in sports and reported from almost every major sporting event since the early 1990s. Working in Chicago, they followed the Bulls every step of the way on their magical run to history during the 1995-96 season. Tom was in the locker room for the majority of their 72 regular season wins while Jon has covered all four Bulls World Championships. During the basketball season Jon has Bulls superstar Dennis Rodman as his regular sidekick on a weekly Sunday Night Sports show.

They have filed live reports and game features from almost all Super Bowls, NBA and Major League All-Star games and NBA Finals during the 90s. Jon covered every single day of the 1996 Summer Olympics in Atlanta and they are no strangers to major college football bowl games and other NCAA Championships.